Brimming with creative inspiration, how-to projects, and useful information to enrich your everyday life, Quarto Knows is a favorite destination for those pursuing their interests and passions. Visit our site and dig deeper with our books into your area of interest: Quarto Creates, Quarto Cooks, Quarto Homes, Quarto Lives, Quarto Drives, Quarto Explores, Quarto Gifts, or Quarto Kids.

Text © 2018 Lily Murray
Illustrations © 2018 Ana Albero

First Published in 2018 by Lincoln Children's Books,
an imprint of The Quarto Group.
400 First Avenue North, Suite 400, Minneapolis, MN 55401, USA.
T (612) 344-8100 F (612) 344-8692 **www.QuartoKnows.com**

The right of Ana Albero to be identified as the illustrator and Lily Murray to be identified as the author of this work has been asserted by them in accordance with the Copyright, Designs and Patents Act, 1988 (United Kingdom).

A catalog record for this book is available from the British Library.

ISBN 978-1-78603-064-1

The illustrations were created in pencil and colored digitally
Set in Gotham Rounded

Published by Jenny Broom and Rachel Williams
Designed by Karissa Santos
Edited by Kate Davies
Production by Catherine Cragg

Manufactured in Guangdong, China CC052018

9 8 7 6 5 4 3 2 1

MIX
Paper from
responsible sources
FSC® C008047

THE PEOPLE AWARDS

Written by Lily Murray
Illustrated by Ana Albero

Lincoln
Children's Books

WELCOME TO
THE PEOPLE AWARDS!

Hurry up! The ceremony is about to begin. We're here to celebrate people throughout history, from all over the world, who have achieved amazing things. There are prizes for people who have made incredible contributions to science, art, sport and music, awards for activists who have stood up for what is right, and trophies for trailblazers who have pushed boundaries, exploring new worlds and new ideas.

Meet the president who brought an end to slavery, and the woman who runs for peace. Learn about the inventor of the bestselling toy of all time, and the famous poet whose words have been lost in time. Find out why they have been given their awards, and what obstacles they had to overcome. Most of all, be inspired by men and women who have pursued their passions.

Now, put your hands together and clap!
The People's Awards is about to begin...

The Nominees for The People Awards are:

 **8** Albert Einstein

 **10** Wangari Maathai

 **12** Abraham Lincoln

 **14** Valentina Tereskova

 **16** Leonardo da Vinci

18
Isaac Newton
Ernö Rubik
Sejong the Great
Jan Amos Komenský

 **20** Marie Curie

 **22** Mahatma Gandhi

 **24** Trischa Zorn

 **26** Pablo Picasso

 **28** J. K. Rowling

30
Hanae Mori
Rudolf Nureyev
Katherine Johnson
Roald Amundsen

 **32** Vincent Lingiari

 **34** Tim Berners-Lee

 **36** Ellen DeGeneres

 **38** Nelson Mandela

 **40** Mary Anning

42
Wolfgang Amadeus Mozart
Antoni Gaudí
Sappho
Hans Christian Andersen

 **44** Alfred Nobel

 **46** Frida Kahlo

 **48** Louis Pasteur

 **50** Gabriel García Márquez

 **52** Olaudah Equiano

54
Antónia Rodrigues
Rigoberta Menchú Tum
Muhammad Ali
Simón Bolívar
Rosa Parks

 **56** David Bowie

 **58** Anne Frank

 **60** Confucius

 **62** Cleopatra

 **64** Pelé

66
Ana Nzinga
Donald Bradman
Eva Perón
Joan of Arc

 **68** Ludwig van Beethoven

 **70** Maria Montessori

 **72** Tegla Loroupe

 **74** Malala Yousafzai

76
The Lap of Honor

ALBERT EINSTEIN

Born: 1849 Died: 1955, Germany/USA
Scientist

Albert Einstein didn't really like school—he found it too strict, and one of his teachers said, "He will never get anywhere in life." But from a young age, he was curious about how the universe worked, and he enjoyed figuring things out for himself.

Albert wanted to be a physics teacher, but he couldn't get a job anywhere, so he ended up working in an office. He studied physics in his spare time and conducted "thought experiments," imagining what it would be like to travel on a beam of light. He used his knowledge and his imagination to come up with amazing theories about light, matter, gravity, space, and time.

In 1919, Albert's idea that gravity could bend light was put to the test...and proved right! It changed how people understood the universe. Albert become world famous overnight, and in 1921, he was awarded the Nobel Prize for Physics.

Albert achieved great things in his life, but he never stopped trying to make sense of the universe, and he never thought of himself as special.

"I have no special talents. I am only passionately curious."
—Albert Einstein

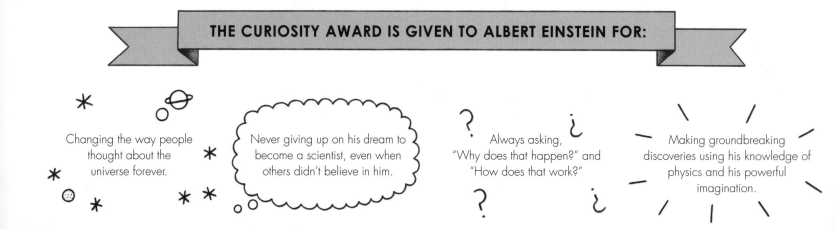

THE CURIOSITY AWARD IS GIVEN TO ALBERT EINSTEIN FOR:

Changing the way people thought about the universe forever.

Never giving up on his dream to become a scientist, even when others didn't believe in him.

Always asking, "Why does that happen?" and "How does that work?"

Making groundbreaking discoveries using his knowledge of physics and his powerful imagination.

When Albert was five years old, his father bought him a compass.
At once, he began trying to figure out why the needle always pointed north.

Albert loved music more than anything else. He took his violin
everywhere with him and named it "Lina."

Einstein came up with the world's most famous equation, $E = mc^2$.
It proves that mass can turn into energy and that energy can turn into mass.

WANGARI MAATHAI

Born: 1940 Died: 2011, Kenya
Activist

Wangari Maathai grew up in the forested mountains of Kenya. Most girls weren't educated, but her parents realized she was very bright and sent her to school. Wangari worked hard, and at the age of 20, she went to study in the United States.

Wangari returned to Kenya as a successful scientist and saw that things were changing in her country—many forests had been chopped down for wood and to make room for coffee plantations. The land was being destroyed, people were hungry, and wildlife was disappearing. So Wangari founded the Green Belt Movement to help women and the environment. She encouraged women all over Kenya to take back their land by planting trees. She knew this would provide them with fuel, shelter, food, and work.

Wangari became known as Mama Miti, "Mother of Trees." She died in 2011, but the Green Belt Movement lives on. So far, over 51 million trees have been planted by women all over Kenya.

"Each of us can make a difference, and together achieve what might seem impossible." —*Wangari Maathai*

THE STAND UP FOR WHAT YOU BELIEVE IN AWARD IS GIVEN TO WANGARI MAATHAI FOR:

Becoming the first female university professor in Kenya, and the first African woman to win a Nobel Prize.

Fighting for women's rights.

Helping to reduce poverty and save forests around the world.

Fighting for democracy and fair elections in Kenya.

As a young girl, Wangari's parents taught her to respect the land and the trees

Wangari wasn't afraid to speak out against her country's ruler, fighting for democracy, women's rights, and the environment, even when it put her life in danger.

In 2004, Wangari was awarded the Nobel Peace Prize, one of the most important prizes in the world. She was the first African woman to win the prize.

Wangari was arrested several times, but she didn't stop fighting.

ABRAHAM LINCOLN

Born: 1809 Died: 1865, USA
President of the United States of America

Abraham Lincoln was born to a poor family of farmers and educated himself by reading every book he could find. He had lots of different jobs—he worked as a shopkeeper, soldier, and lawyer. Then, when he was 25, he became a politician.

In 1860, Abraham ran for president of the United States—and he won! He was determined to end slavery, because he had seen how hard life was for slaves in the Southern states. But lots of people in the South didn't want to give up their slaves and didn't want Abraham as their president. Eleven states decided to leave the United States, but Abraham vowed to keep the country together, even if it meant war. A civil war broke out between the North and South and lasted for over four years. Eventually the Southern states were defeated.

Abraham had suceeded in ending slavery and keeping the United States united. Now he wanted to heal the divisions between the two halves of the country. Sadly, he didn't live to see that happen. Soon after the end of the war, on a trip to the theater, he was shot and killed by a supporter of slavery. He is remembered as one of the United States' greatest presidents.

The **STOPPING SLAVERY** *Award*

"Those who deny freedom to others deserve it not for themselves." —*Abraham Lincoln*

THE STOPPING SLAVERY AWARD IS GIVEN TO ABRAHAM LINCOLN FOR:

Abolishing slavery in the United States.

Becoming president of the United States against the odds.

Keeping the United States of America together.

Wearing an amazing hat. It was so big that he used to keep letters in it.

When Abraham was 19, he was hired to steer a boat down the Mississippi River. This trip to the Southern states opened his eyes to the horrors of slavery.

In 1863, Abraham made an order, known as the Emancipation Proclamation, ordering that all slaves in the Southern states should be freed. This order eventually freed millions of slaves.

On November 19, 1863, Abraham gave a great speech, known as the Gettysburg Address, talking about the struggle for all people to be equal.

Abraham loved animals and had lots of pets including dogs, cats, horses, goats, and a turkey named Jack. Jack was supposed to be eaten for Christmas dinner, but Abraham's son persuaded him to save the turkey's life.

VALENTINA TERESHKOVA

Born: 1937, Russia
Cosmonaut (the Russian name for astronaut), pilot, engineer

Valentina Tereshkova loved studying, but she had to leave school at 16 to earn money in a textile factory. She studied in her spare time, though, and she took up parachuting as a hobby. When she discovered that her country was planning to send the first woman into space, she immediately applied. Because she knew how to parachute, she was one of five out of 400 women to be chosen.

Valentina trained hard for months to prepare for her mission. Her spaceship, *Vostok 6*, blasted off on June 16, 1963, and Valentina became the first woman in space. In that single flight, lasting almost three days, Valentina orbited the earth 48 times. She kept a logbook, recording what it was like to be in space, and took photos of the moon. She'd forgotten her toothbrush, so she had to brush her teeth with her fingers. Valentina never flew into space again, but became an engineer and worked in the government. She won many awards, including the United Nations Gold Medal of Peace. A crater on the far side of the moon is named after her—the Tereshkova crater.

"Hey, sky, take off your hat! I'm coming to see you."
—Valentina Tereshkova

THE SPACE WOMAN AWARD IS GIVEN TO VALENTINA TERESHKOVA FOR:

Being the first woman in space— and the only woman ever to fly into space alone.

Inspiring women to become cosmonauts, astronauts, and scientists.

Fighting for women's rights.

Volunteering to go on a one-way mission to Mars if a Mars mission ever takes place—even though she's over 80!

Before Valentina could go into space, she had to learn to fly jet fighters and how to fix any problems with her spacecraft.

After launching, Valentina spotted a fault in Vostok 6's computer program that meant the rocket would spin endlessly away from Earth and never take her home. She kept calm and reported it to ground control, who fixed it.

Valentina spoke to President Nikita Khrushchev from space, and a television camera inside her capsule broadcast her mission live on television.

When Vostok 6 was coming back to Earth, it hurtled through Earth's atmosphere at 17,000 miles per hour. Valentina was ejected from her capsule 4 miles above the surface and parachuted safely back to land.

LEONARDO DA VINCI

Born: 1452 Died: 1519, Italy
Inventor, artist, scientist, engineer

Even as a child, Leonardo was a talented artist. At age 14, he became an apprentice to one of the finest artists in Florence. He learned drawing and painting as well as chemistry, carpentry, and metalwork. At the age of 26, Leonardo set up a studio of his own.

But Leonardo wasn't only interested in art. He kept notebooks full of drawings of inventions. He drew machines that looked like bicycles, parachutes, and helicopters. Most of the things he drew weren't actually made for hundreds of years.

As an adult, Leonardo moved around, working for the ruling families of the day. In Milan, he designed a dome for the cathedral and an armored tank. He also painted *The Last Supper*, one of the world's most famous paintings, showing Jesus's last meal with his followers. In Florence, Leonardo designed plans to protect the city from invasion. He ended his days working for Francis I, the king of France. One of his last works was an amazing mechanical walking lion that opened its chest to reveal a bouquet of lilies and flowers.

The **GOOD AT EVERYTHING** *Award*

"He who thinks little makes lots of mistakes."
—*Leonardo da Vinci*

THE GOOD AT EVERYTHING AWARD IS GIVEN TO LEONARDO DA VINCI FOR:

Painting some of the world's most famous works of art.

Inventing things that were so ahead of their time that they weren't actually made for hundreds of years.

Being a brilliant engineer and scientist as well as an artist.

Realizing that studying science made him a better artist, and studying art made him a better scientist.

Leonardo learned by observing the world around him. He spent hours watching birds in order to create designs for flying machines.

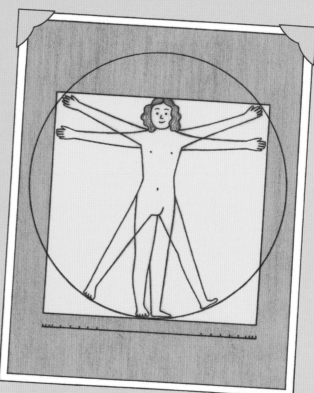

Leonardo also studied the human body in detail and drew a famous sketch called The Vitruvian Man, a picture of a man with perfect proportions.

In 1503, Leonardo began work on his most famous painting of all, the Mona Lisa, a portrait of a woman with a mysterious smile.

Leonardo was left-handed and wrote back to front, from right to left across the page, so that his notes could only be read using a mirror. He may have done this to keep his ideas secret.

The BRILLIANT IDEA Awards

It's time for the Brilliant Idea Awards—let's celebrate people who have changed the world with fantastic ideas and inventions.

ISAAC NEWTON

Best Idea from Looking at an Apple Award

Born: 1642 Died: 1727, UK
Scientist, mathematician, astronomer

Isaac Newton discovered gravity, the force that pulls everything toward Earth. He said his discovery was inspired by watching an apple fall from a tree outside his house.

ERNÖ RUBIK

The Magic Cube Award

Born: 1944, Hungary
Inventor, architect, professor

Ernö was an architecture teacher when he made the first Rubik's cube as a puzzle for his students. It was launched as a toy in 1979, and over 350 million have been sold.

JAN AMOS KOMENSKÝ
The Best Teacher Award

Born: 1592 Died: 1670, Netherlands/Czech Republic
Teacher, educator, philosopher, writer

Jan wanted to make sure everyone had access to an education. He introduced pictures in textbooks and said books should be written in the languages people spoke—before he came along, schoolbooks were in Latin!

SEJONG THE GREAT
The Brand New Alphabet Award

Born: 1397 Died: 1450, Korea
King of the Joseon dynasty, Korea

Sejong the Great was a king who wanted to improve the lives of his subjects. He invented Hangul, the simple, 28-letter Korean alphabet, so that all Koreans could learn to read and write.

MARIE CURIE

Born: 1867 Died: 1934
Scientist

Marie was born in Poland, the youngest of five children. Her parents were teachers who gave their children a love of learning, but life was hard. Marie's mother and one of her sisters died before she was ten, and they often struggled for money.

Marie and her sister, Bronia, made a pact to help each other. First Marie worked as a governess so Bronia could train as a doctor, then Bronia helped pay for Marie to study at the Sorbonne University in Paris. At the Sorbonne, Marie met Pierre Curie, a fellow scientist, and they married a year later. Together, they investigated invisible rays called radioactivity. They also discovered two new elements. But they didn't realize that the radiation from these elements was dangerous.

Then, in 1906, Pierre was killed in a street accident. Marie was devastated, but she kept working hard and took over Pierre's job, becoming the first woman to teach at the Sorbonne. She died from a disease caused by radiation. She and Pierre were buried in the Panthéon in Paris, the resting place of France's greatest citizens.

The **X-RAY** *Award*

"Nothing in life is to be feared; it is only to be understood." —Marie Curie

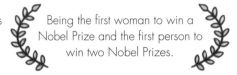

THE X-RAY AWARD IS GIVEN TO MARIE CURIE FOR:

 Being one of the most famous scientists of all time. She was often refused jobs because she was a woman, but she never gave up.

 For discovering two new elements of the periodic table—polonium and radium.

Being the first woman to win a Nobel Prize and the first person to win two Nobel Prizes.

Founding the Curie Institutes in Paris and in Warsaw, which are still important places of medical research today.

MAHATMA GANDHI

Born: 1869 Died: 1948, India
Activist

Gandhi was born in India to a wealthy family, but his mother taught him to live a simple life. He was a Hindu, and he believed that people of different faiths should live together peacefully and respect each other's religions.

Gandhi trained as a lawyer and went to work in South Africa. When he saw how Indian people were treated there, he started "nonviolent protests"—a way of fighting peacefully to stand up for people's rights. When Gandhi returned home, he led the fight for India's independence from the British Empire. So many people took part in the protests that it brought the whole country to a halt. The British put him in prison for his protests, but he fought back by refusing to eat, so eventually they had to let him go. Gandhi soon became a hero in his own country.

In 1947, Gandhi's campaign succeeded, and India became an independent country. But, months later, he was killed by a man who was angry with him for arguing that people of all religions should be equal. Today, Gandhi is remembered all over the world as a great and peaceful leader.

"Equal freedom for all."
—Mahatma Gandhi

THE BE THE CHANGE AWARD IS GIVEN TO MAHATMA GANDHI FOR:

Inspiring many people around the world to fight against unfairness.

Promoting peace between people of all religions.

Using nonviolent ways to fight for people's freedom.

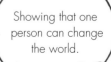
Showing that one person can change the world.

In South Africa, Gandhi began to live even more simply than before. He started dressing in a white cloth, called a dhoti. In 1914, he was given the honorific name "Mahatma," which means someone who is loved and respected.

In 1930, Gandhi led a 241-mile "Salt March" to the sea, in protest at the high salt tax the British charged Indian people. Thousands joined him, and Britain was forced to give in to Gandhi's demands.

Gandhi encouraged people to protest against the British Empire, which ruled India at the time, by refusing to work and sitting in the streets instead.

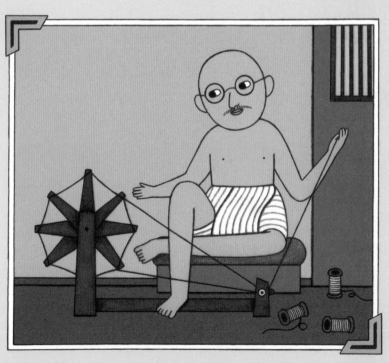

In prison, Gandhi used a spinning wheel to spin thread and make his own clothes. He kept spinning throughout his life, and the wheel become a symbol of the Indian independence movement.

TRISCHA ZORN

Born: 1964, USA
Swimmer, paralympian

Trischa was born blind, but she never let that get in her way. She found school hard as she had to rely on her hearing for everything she learned, but from the moment she took up swimming she loved the freedom it gave her. At the age of 16, she competed in her first Paralympic Games, winning seven gold medals and setting three world records.

Trischa went on to win six more titles in the 1984 Paralympics, and added 12 more in Seoul in 1988. She remained unbeaten in her races until 1992. When she wasn't competing or training, Trischa worked as a school teacher so that she could pass on what she had learned to inner-city children. She finished her amazing swimming career at the age of 40 by winning a bronze medal in the women's 100-metre backstroke at the 2004 Paralympic Games.

Trisha now works as a coach, lawyer and teacher. She still helps others, encouraging wounded American servicemen and women to get into para-sport.

"Records are meant to be broken." —Trischa Zorn

THE AMAZING ATHLETE AWARD IS GIVEN TO TRISCHA ZORN FOR:

Being the most successful athlete in the history of the Paralympic Games.

 Competing in seven Paralympic Games, from Arnhem in 1980 to Athens in 2004.

 Winning 55 medals (41 gold, nine silver, and five bronze).

Inspiring young women and disabled athletes to compete and let nothing stand in their way.

Trischa first took up swimming at the age of ten, joining the Mission Viejo swim club in Southern California.

ATHENS 2004   ATHENS 2004

Trischa's mother died shortly before the 2004 Paralympic Games in Athens. Even though Trischa was very sad and missed her mother terribly, she went on to come in third. Of all her medals, her bronze at Athens is the one of which she is most proud.

PABLO PICASSO

Born: 1881 Died: 1973, Spain
Artist

Pablo Picasso grew up in Spain. His father was an art teacher, and he soon realized that Pablo was brilliant at art. He could draw and paint just about anything, in any style.

When Pablo was 14, he went to a famous art school in Barcelona, but found his lessons boring. He didn't want to paint like everyone else—he wanted to create a new kind of art. So, at the age of 23, he moved to Paris, where exciting new things were happening in the art world. Three years later, Pablo and his friend, Georges Braque, developed a new type of painting called Cubism. They looked at an object from many different angles and then put all the views together in one painting, so that the picture looked like it was made up of different fragments.

Pablo never painted in one style for long and kept experimenting with art his whole life. During the early years of his career, he painted in blue to show his feelings of sadness, then as he grew happier he began his "Rose Period," painting in brighter colors. He tried out collage—sticking newspapers and material to his paintings—as well as sculpture, classical painting, and childlike paintings. Pablo kept working right up until the day he died, believing that somehow his work would keep him alive.

"All children are artists. The problem is how to remain an artist once you grow up." —Pablo Picasso

THE SHAKING UP ART AWARD IS GIVEN TO PABLO PICASSO FOR:

Creating *Les Demoiselles d'Avignon* in 1907, a painting like no one had ever seen before.

Coming up with many new styles of art, including Cubism and collage.

Spending his whole life creating. Picasso produced 1,885 paintings, 2,880 ceramics, 1,228 sculptures, and around 12,000 drawings.

Being one of the creators of modern art, changing the way people thought about art forever.

J. K. ROWLING

Born: 1965, UK
Writer

J. K. Rowling's real name is Joanne. She grew up in Gloucestershire, England, and always loved writing stories, which she would read aloud to her younger sister. Her first book was about a rabbit named Rabbit, which she wrote at age six. Joanne says that as a child she always had her nose in a book and wore large glasses, just like one of her characters, Hermione Granger.

After school, Joanne went to college and then worked for a charity. But at the age of 25, on a long train journey, she had an idea for a story about a boy wizard. Over the next few years, she kept writing the story, even when she had a small baby and was very poor.

Five years later, Joanne finished *Harry Potter and the Sorcerer's Stone* and sent it out to publishers. Twelve turned it down, but one agreed to take it on. It became a huge success, and Joanne went on to write six more Harry Potter books. They have become the fastest-selling books in history, translated into 65 languages and loved by children all over the world.

"We do not need magic to change the world, we carry all the power we need inside ourselves already: we have the power to imagine better." —J.K. Rowling

THE MOST MAGICAL MUGGLE AWARD IS GIVEN TO J.K. ROWLING FOR:

Creating the magical world of Harry Potter, in which "Muggles" are non-magic people.

Keeping going even when she felt she was a failure.

Giving huge amounts to charity and working hard to help others.

Inspiring children all over the world to read.

At age 11, Joanne wrote her first novel,
about seven cursed diamonds.

Joanne has also written crime novels for grown-ups.
At first, her identity was a secret, as she wrote under
the name Robert Galbraith.

In 2001, Joanne married again and had two more children,
David and Mackenzie. She built a magical Hogwarts tree
house for them at their home in Scotland.

The final book of the Harry Potter series, Harry Potter and the
Deathly Hallows, *became the fastest-selling book of all time, with
11 million copies sold on its first day of release.*

The **TRAILBLAZER** *Awards*

We are proud to present the Trailblazer Awards! These brilliant people led the way in their careers and inspired others who followed in their footsteps.

HANAE MORI
The Fantastic Fashion Award

Born: 1926, Japan
Fashion designer

Hanae took classes at a local dressmaking school. After a visit to Paris, she started to design clothes, using a butterfly as her symbol. Her designs appeared on the cover of *Vogue* magazine and became very popular. She has also designed costumes for movies, operas, and clothes for the Olympics.

RUDOLF NUREYEV
The Beautiful Dancer Award

Born: 1938 Died: 1993, Russia/France
Dancer, producer, choreographer, film star

Born to a poor peasant family, Rudolf knew he wanted to be a dancer from the time he first saw the opera. He began studying ballet at the age of 11 and, after graduating, he joined the top ballet company in Russia, the Kirov Ballet. Three years later, on a company tour, he fled the Communist-controlled country and moved to Paris. He became one of the most famous ballet dancers in the world, known for the passion and energy he brought to his roles.

ROALD AMUNDSEN
The Intrepid Explorer Award

Born: 1872 Died: 1928, Norway
Explorer

Roald always longed to explore wild places, and he joined his first Antarctic expedition as first mate at the age of 25. When the ship became stuck in the sea ice, they became the first expedition to survive winter in Antarctica. In 1911, Roald became the first man to reach the South Pole, leading a team of men using skis and sled dogs. Sadly, Roald died after his plane crashed in Arctic fog during a rescue mission. His body was never found.

KATHERINE JOHNSON
The Shoot for the Stars Award

Born: 1918, USA
Physicist, mathematician

Katherine worked for a space agency (now NASA). At first, as an African American, she had to work in a different room from white people, and women weren't given credit for their work. But Katherine was so good at her job she couldn't be ignored. She calculated the path of space flights for many missions and, in 2015, was awarded with the Presidential Medal of Freedom.

VINCENT LINGIARI

Born: 1919 Died: 1988, Australia
Activitist

Vincent was born into the Gurindji community, a group of indigenous people in Australia (people descended from those who originally lived in Australia).

Vincent never went to school and, at the age of 12, he started work, looking after cattle. He worked on land that had traditionally belonged to his people but that had been taken over by white settlers. It was hard work, and indigenous workers weren't paid properly.

By the age of 47, Vincent had become an important leader in the Gurindji community and decided to take action at the way his people were being treated. He led 200 workers in a walkout to show how they felt about their terrible conditions. They stopped work and demanded better pay as well as the return of some of their traditional lands. The strike lasted for nine years.

Throughout the struggle, Vincent was known for his quiet dignity and for never giving up. Eventually, Lingiari and his people won and their lands were returned to them. Vincent became a national hero.

The
NEVER GIVE UP
Award

"We want to live on our land, our way."
—*Vincent Lingiari*

THE NEVER GIVE UP AWARD IS GIVEN TO VINCENT LINGIARI FOR:

Standing up for what he knew was right.

Gathering support from people all across Australia for his cause.

Having a vision. Vincent wanted his people to have an education, clean water, and electricity, and to be able to run their own cattle ranches.

Fighting for a change in the law. His people now have a right to their land and to practice their own laws and culture.

Working at the cattle ranch, Vincent was in charge of 80,000 cattle, but received no money for his work.

After the strike, Vincent traveled across Australia to tell everyone about the struggles faced by his people and to win support for indigenous people's rights.

In 1975, the prime minister of Australia poured the local sand into Vincent's hands to show that he was handing land back to the Gurindji people. Vincent then said, "Now we can all be mates."

In 1976, the Aboriginal Land Rights Act was passed, which gave indigenous Australians the rights to their lands in the Northern Territory of Australia. That year, Vincent was named a Member of the Order of Australia.

TIM BERNERS-LEE

Born: 1955, UK
Computer scientist, inventor of the World Wide Web

Tim grew up in London as one of four children. From a young age, Tim was fascinated by computers. He also loved trains and first learned about electronics while playing with his model trains.

After school, Tim studied physics at Oxford University. By the age of 25, he was working at CERN, a famous center for scientific research in Switzerland. Part of his job involved sharing information with scientists all over the world, and he worked with hypertext, a language that allows you to share information electronically.

Tim figured out how to join hypertext with the internet, creating a system for sharing information around the world. He named it the World Wide Web, and it went online in 1991.

As the World Wide Web grew, Tim set up an organization to oversee how the Web developed and work to improve it. Today, he speaks out against governments who censor the Web, trying to stop people from finding out certain information. In 2012, Tim played a starring role in the opening ceremony for the Olympics, tweeting, "This is for everyone."

"The Web does not just connect machines, it connects people." —*Tim Berners-Lee*

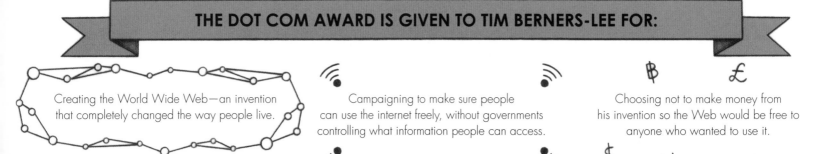

THE DOT COM AWARD IS GIVEN TO TIM BERNERS-LEE FOR:

Creating the World Wide Web—an invention that completely changed the way people live.

Campaigning to make sure people can use the internet freely, without governments controlling what information people can access.

Choosing not to make money from his invention so the Web would be free to anyone who wanted to use it.

Tim began inventing things when he was 11, first making electronic gadgets to control his model trains.

On August 6, 1991, Tim launched the world's first website, http://info.cern.ch. It explained the World Wide Web and gave users all over the world an introduction to making their own websites.

Tim has received many awards and honours, including Knight Commander of the Order of the British Empire, and the Order of Merit, which is given by the queen to just 24 living people.

ELLEN DEGENERES

Born: 1958, USA
Comedian, television host, actor, writer, producer

Ellen always wanted to be famous. When she was 23, she started doing stand-up comedy in small clubs and cafés. She was spotted by an agent and became the first female comedian to be invited on set by a famous TV show host named Johnny Carson. Then she starred in her own TV show, a sitcom called *Ellen*.

In 1997, at the peak of her fame, Ellen announced on national television that she was a lesbian. The character she played on TV also came out as gay. No American celebrity had ever announced that they were gay to so many viewers. It was a very brave thing to do, as there was a lot more homophobia (discrimination against gay people) at the time, and she didn't know how her fans would react. Some advertisers stopped supporting Ellen's show and it was canceled— but Ellen didn't give up. In 2003, she starred in *Finding Nemo* and launched her own talk show, which became a huge success. In 2016, Ellen received the Presidential Medal of Freedom, an important honor, from President Barack Obama. He said that by coming out, Ellen had paved the way for equal rights for LGBT (lesbian, gay, bisexual, and transgender) people and that she "reminds us that we have more in common than we realize."

The
**LOVE IS
LOVE**
Award

"Stay true to yourself. Have your own opinion."
—*Ellen DeGeneres*

THE LOVE IS LOVE AWARD IS GIVEN TO ELLEN DEGENERES FOR:

Announcing to the world that she was gay, even though it meant risking her career.

Becoming the first openly gay person to play a gay main character on television.

Hosting a multi-award-winning talk show that's been on the air for over 15 years.

Supporting and raising millions of dollars for charities.

Ellen's first big break came in 1982, when she entered
a national talent contest with her stand-up act. She won
the title of "Funniest Person in America."

In 2007, Ellen became the first openly gay or lesbian
person to host the Oscars®.

When President Obama gave Ellen her Medal of Freedom award,
he called her a "role model" for Americans.

In 2008, Ellen married her partner, actress
Portia de Rossi, at their home in Los Angeles.

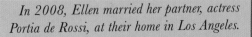

NELSON MANDELA

Born: 1918 Died: 2013, South Africa
Activist, President of South Africa

Mandela's birth name was Rolihlahla, which means "troublemaker." When he was seven, a teacher gave him the nickname "Nelson." He did well in school and loved boxing and running. After school, he went to college to study law. At that time, Nelson's country, South Africa, did not treat black and white people equally. Most black people were poor and worked as servants or on farms and in factories. Only white people were allowed in government, so black people had no say in how the country was run.

In 1944, Nelson joined the African National Congress (ANC) to work toward black South Africans having the same rights as white South Africans. Four years later, the government changed the law to a system called "apartheid" to keep black people and white people apart. Mandela and another lawyer set up South Africa's first black law firm and helped many poor people. Nelson also spoke out against apartheid, but in 1962, Nelson was arrested and sent to prison for life.

"It always seems impossible until it's done."
—*Nelson Mandela*

THE FIGHT FOR FREEDOM AWARD IS GIVEN TO NELSON MANDELA FOR:

Fighting for black people to be treated equally, even though it meant he spent 27 years in prison.

Being leader of a secret army, the "Spear of the Nation," that fought for black people's rights.

Becoming the first black president of South Africa.

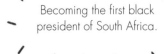

As president, working tirelessly for human rights and a better future for everyone in South Africa.

Nelson grew up in a small South African village. His father was a tribal chief, and Nelson was a member of the Thembu royal family.

At the age of 23, Nelson ran away to Johannesburg to avoid an arranged marriage. There, he saw for the first time how hard life was for many black South Africans.

At age 46, Mandela was sent to a prison called Robben Island. He spent 18 years there. He was forced to do incredibly hard work and was only allowed one visitor every six months.

In 1993, Nelson Mandela and F. W. de Klerk, the president who had ordered his release from prison, were jointly awarded the Nobel Peace Prize.

MARY ANNING

Born: 1799 Died: 1847, UK
Fossil collector, paleontologist (dinosaur scientist)

Born to a poor family, Mary was one of nine children, but only she and her brother Joseph lived past childhood. She taught herself to read and write and helped her father on his fossil-hunting trips along the coastline where they lived.

When Mary was 11, her father died falling from a cliff, leaving the family poorer than ever. Joseph and Mary kept hunting for fossils to sell and, a year later, Joseph found a skull sticking out of a rock. Mary kept searching, carefully chipping away at the rock with a hammer. She uncovered the first complete skeleton of an Ichthyosaurus, a sea reptile that lived at the same time as the dinosaurs.

Mary went on to discover more and more amazing fossils. Scientists from all over Europe and America came to talk to her about her work. But Mary lived at a time when women weren't allowed to vote or attend college. Male scientists published the scientific descriptions of the fossils she found and often they didn't even mention her name.

The fossils Mary found changed the way scientists thought about prehistoric life. Her fame grew after her death and in 2010, the Royal Society (the UK academy of science) included Mary Anning in a list of ten British women who have most influenced the history of science.

The **FOSSIL HUNTER** *Award*

"She sells seashells on the seashore."
—a famous tongue twister inspired by Mary Anning

THE FOSSIL HUNTER AWARD IS GIVEN TO MARY ANNING FOR:

Changing the way scientists thought about prehistoric life.

 Realizing that strange rocks known as bezoar stones were actually fossilized dinosaur poop.

 Making a name for herself as a scientist at a time when almost all scientists were men.

 Bravely carrying out dangerous work in the name of science.

Mary discovered the first two skeletons of plesiosaurs, huge marine reptiles that lived at the same time as the dinosaurs.

Because Mary was a woman, she wasn't allowed to join the important scientific societies of the day.

Mary often went fossil hunting in the winter months when fierce storms exposed new fossils. In 1833, she nearly died during a landslide that killed her faithful dog, Tray.

The CREATIVITY Awards

Here's to the creatives—the artists, writers, musicians, and architects who make beautiful works of art that bring joy to millions of people!

WOLFGANG AMADEUS MOZART

The Child Prodigy Award

Born: 1756 Died: 1791, Austria
Composer, musician

Mozart was one of the greatest composers of all time. His most famous works include *The Magic Flute, Don Giovanni,* and *The Marriage of Figaro*. By the age of five, he could write his own musical compositions and by six, he was touring Europe, performing for royalty.

ANTONI GAUDÍ

The Weird and Wonderful Buildings Award

Born: 1852 Died: 1926, Spain
Architect

Antoni Gaudí designed incredible buildings in Barcelona, Spain. He covered them in colored tiles and gave them swirling, curving lines inspired by nature. His most famous works include Park Güell, Casa Batlló, Casa Milà, and the Sagrada Família.

HANS CHRISTIAN ANDERSEN

The Everlasting Stories Award

Born: 1805 Died: 1875, Denmark
Writer

Hans Christian Andersen left school at a young age to earn money as a tailor. But at age 17, he was able to go back to school, and after leaving, he wrote some of the world's most famous fairy tales—*The Emperor's New Clothes*, *The Little Mermaid*, *The Snow Queen*, *The Ugly Duckling*, *The Princess and the Pea*, and *Thumbelina*.

SAPPHO

The Lost Love Poems Award

Born: c. 630 BC Died: c. 580 BC, Greece
Poet

Sappho was a famous poet in her day who wrote simple but passionate poems about her love for both men and women. Her fame survived through the ages, but most of her work did not. All that is left are tiny scraps and fragments, and one 28-line poem.

ALFRED NOBEL

Born: 1833 Died: 1896, Sweden/Italy
Scientist, inventor, businessman, founder of the Nobel Prizes

Alfred was born in Sweden, but when he was nine, his family moved to Russia. There, Alfred and his four brothers were given an excellent education. They learned science, literature, and languages, and by the age of 17, Alfred could speak Swedish, Russian, French, English, and German.

Alfred moved back to Sweden to become a scientist, working on explosives. But, in 1864, a huge blast in one of his family's weapons factories killed five people, including his younger brother, Emil. After that, Alfred was determined to find a safer type of explosive.

In 1866, at the age of 36, he developed one: dynamite. Alfred became very rich. But in 1888, a French paper published Alfred's obituary by accident with the title "The Merchant of Death Is Dead." Alfred was very upset that he was going to be remembered for inventing something that caused destruction. He changed his will and declared that almost all of his fortune should be used to set up the Nobel Prizes. These are given each year to those who have made the greatest achievements throughout the world.

"If I have a thousand ideas and only one turns out to be good, I am satisfied." —Alfred Nobel

THE GIVING OUT PRIZES AWARD IS GIVEN TO ALFRED NOBEL FOR:

Leaving his fortune to create the Nobel Prizes.

Setting up the Nobel Peace Prize to encourage people and organizations to work for peace.

Wanting to help people after his death.

Loving books and reading, as well science, and making sure there was also a Nobel Prize for writing.

Alfred's invention, dynamite, has been used to blast tunnels, cut canals, and build railways and roads all over the world.

Although he was a scientist, Alfred loved books and also wrote poetry, novels, and a play.

One of Alfred's secretaries, Bertha von Suttner, later became very active in the peace movement. She and Alfred remained friends, and she helped him think about the importance of peace. Because of her, Alfred included a prize for persons or organizations who worked for peace.

FRIDA KAHLO

Born: 1907 Died: 1954, Mexico
Artist

Frida grew up in Mexico. At the age of six, she caught a disease called polio, which damaged her right leg and left her with a limp. She went to school, worked hard, and studied to be a doctor, but then, when she was 18, she was in a terrible bus accident. She broke many of the bones in her body and was in constant pain for the rest of her life.

While Frida was recovering, she began to paint. She finished her first self-portrait the following year. In 1928, she met a well-known Mexican artist named Diego Rivera and asked him what he thought of her art. He encouraged her to pursue her talent, and they married the following year.

Frida's work was often very personal, showing what was happening to her and how she was feeling. She painted pictures of herself at important moments in her life. Her paintings show her when she was lonely and in pain, and reflected her sadness that she couldn't have children. Today Frida is thought of as an inspirational woman who was both creative and brave.

"Feet, what do I need you for when I have wings to fly?" —Frida Kahlo

THE PAINTING THROUGH PAIN AWARD IS GIVEN TO FRIDA KAHLO FOR:

Painting throughout her life, even though she was in constant pain.

Becoming one of the most important woman artists in history.

Speaking out for women's rights and those of indigenous Mexicans.

Painting the casts and corsets she had to wear so they became works of art rather than just medical equipment.

Frida grew up in the house where she was born, now known as the Blue House, or Casa Azul. Today it is a museum dedicated to Frida's life and work.

Frida was also well known for her brightly colored clothes and jewelry. From a young age, she wore traditional Mexican Tehuana clothes with long skirts. These showed her support for indigenous Mexicans and helped hide her injured leg.

In 1939, Frida went to live in Paris. There she exhibited her paintings and became friends with famous artists, including Picasso.

In 1953, at the age of 46, Frida had her first solo exhibition in Mexico. Even though she was very ill, she went to the exhibition's opening by ambulance and spent the evening chatting to guests and celebrating in a four-poster bed set up in the gallery.

LOUIS PASTEUR

Born: 1822 Died: 1895, France
Scientist

As a child, Louis wasn't particularly good at schoolwork and preferred drawing and painting. His father didn't want his son to become an artist, however, and made sure Louis worked hard at all his subjects.

Louis went on to study science at university and became a professor. He had five children, but three died young from disease. The loss of his children drove Louis to find cures for infectious diseases. One of Louis' first achievements was to show that germs (bacteria) didn't just appear out of nowhere, as most people thought at the time, but were living things. His work on 'germ theory' led to the development of antiseptics to treat germs and changed healthcare forever. Then, in 1863, Louis made another discovery. He realized that by heating up liquids such as wine or milk, he could kill the germs in them, making them safer to drink. This process became known as pasteurization and is still used today.

Louis continued to investigate diseases. He found that giving people a weak form of a disease could protect them against the actual disease. He called this weak form a 'vaccine' and went on to develop vaccines for many different illnesses.

"In the field of observation, chance favors the prepared mind." —Louis Pasteur

THE SAVING LIVES AWARD IS GIVEN TO LOUIS PASTEUR FOR:

Developing vaccines to protect millions of people from diseases.

Proving that germs cause disease, which changed the way doctors treat people.

Finding new ways to make food safe to eat.

Setting up the Pasteur Institute, one of the leading centers of research in battling infectious diseases.

In 1865, Louis was asked to help save France's silk businesses, after its silkworms were struck by disease. Louis and his wife, Marie, discovered that the silkworm infections were spread by tiny life-forms called parasites. He showed how to remove the infected worms to stop the spread of the disease.

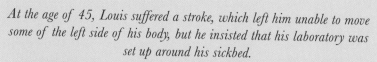

At the age of 45, Louis suffered a stroke, which left him unable to move some of the left side of his body, but he insisted that his laboratory was set up around his sickbed.

On July 6, 1885, Pasteur vaccinated Joseph Meister, a nine-year-old boy who had been bitten by a rabid dog. The vaccine saved the boy's life. It was the first time the rabies vaccine had been used, and it made Louis famous all over the world.

On November 14, 1888, after a long fund-raising campaign, Louis opened the Pasteur Institute in Paris, which was set up to research infectious diseases. Work at the institute has saved millions of lives and still goes on today.

GABRIEL GARCÍA MÁRQUEZ

Born: 1927 Died: 2014, Colombia/Mexico
Writer

Gabriel was the eldest of 11 children. During the first years of his life, he lived with his grandfather, but when his grandfather died, he went to live with his parents. It was a difficult time, as his parents were almost strangers to him.

Gabriel studied law, but then realized he wanted to be a writer. He published his first short story when he was at college and then became a journalist, at a time when there was a lot of violence in his country. In 1955, after writing an article that criticized the government, he was forced to move to Europe. He spent the next few years desperately poor, living in Rome and Paris, and visiting Eastern Europe before returning home.

Then, in the 1960s, while living in Mexico City, he began to write his longest story yet. Published in 1967, his novel *One Hundred Years of Solitude* sold millions of copies all over the world. It was a strange mixture of the ordinary along with magic and fantasy—a style called "magic realism"—and it changed the way people wrote stories. Gabriel wrote five more brilliant novels and lots of shorter books, too. In 1982, he was awarded the Nobel Prize for Literature.

"It is not true that people stop pursuing dreams because they grow old, they grow old because they stop pursuing dreams." —*Gabriel García Márquez*

THE MAGICAL WRITING AWARD IS GIVEN TO GABRIEL GARCÍA MÁRQUEZ FOR:

 Writing articles for newspapers to show what was happening in his country and around the world, even when it put his life at risk.

 Speaking out about poverty and the struggles people in his country faced under terrible leaders.

 Helping introduce South American books and writers to the rest of the world.

 Inspiring lots of great writers to use magic in their stories.

As a child, Gabriel told stories by drawing rather than writing. Before he could read or write, he drew comics at school and at home.

At the age of 31, Gabriel married his childhood sweetheart Mercedes Barcha in Barranquilla, Colombia. They had first met when he was 18 and she was 13 and had written to each other while he was away traveling.

On June 26, 1961, Gabriel and his family arrived at a railway station in Mexico City. They only had $20. Gabriel began writing One Hundred Years of Solitude and finished it 18 months later.

One Hundred Years of Solitude sold out in its first week and has gone on to sell more than 30 million copies around the world, translated into more than 30 languages. After its publication, Gabriel became famous around the world.

OLAUDAH EQUIANO

Born: c. 1745 Died: 1797, Essaka, West Africa/UK
Former slave, merchant, writer, anti-slavery campaigner

Olaudah was born in what is now Nigeria. When he was 11, he and his sister were kidnapped and sold to slave traders. Olaudah was separated from his sister and taken across to Barbados on a slave ship.

Olaudah was sold to Michael Pascal, an officer in the British Royal Navy, who renamed him Gustavus Vassa. For eight years, Olaudah traveled the oceans with Pascal. During that time, he learned to read and write. Pascal promised to free Olaudah, but instead he sold him again. Olaudah's final "owner" allowed him to trade and earn money for himself. In 1767, after 12 years as a slave, Olaudah had earned enough money to buy his freedom. He wrote, "this was the happiest day I had ever experienced."

As a free man, Olaudah lived in London, but spent 20 years sailing from the Arctic to America as a merchant and explorer. He wrote a book called *The Interesting Narrative of the Life of Olaudah Equiano* about his experiences as a slave. It became a bestseller in many different countries and showed the true horror of slavery. Olaudah used the money from his book to fight against slavery and help the poor black people of London. Ten years after his death, the British slave trade was abolished.

"I who had been a slave in the morning…became my own master, and completely free."
—*Olaudah Equiano*

THE KIDNAPPED HERO AWARD IS GIVEN TO OLAUDAH EQUIANO FOR:

Writing a book about his life as a slave so people knew the full horror of slavery.

Being one of the first black African writers in England to have a book published.

Campaigning to end slavery and showing people in England that slavery was wrong.

Olaudah was terrified on board the slave ship that took him from his home, where the slaves were forced into cramped spaces below the decks.

Olaudah had to follow his master Pascal into battle during Britain's Seven Years' War with France. One of his jobs was to bring gunpowder up to the gun decks.

Olaudah spent the last years of his life touring Britain and Ireland, speaking at large public meetings to let everyone know how terrible it was being a slave.

After he was freed, Olaudah married an English woman named Susannah and they had two daughters.

The BRAVERY Awards

Bravery isn't just about fighting—speaking out against injustice and standing up for what you believe in can take as much courage as going into battle.

ANTÓNIA RODRIGUES

The Brave Knight Award

Born: 1580 Died: 1641, Portugal
Knight

António disguised herself as a boy when she was just 12 years old and ran away from home to fight for her country in North Africa. She was brilliant in battle, but when the daughter of a nobleman fell in love with her, believing that she was a man, she had to admit she was a woman and return home. The king of Portugal awarded her with medals for bravery, and she became famous as the "Portuguese knight."

RIGOBERTA MENCHÚ TUM

The Speaking Out Award

Born: 1959, Guatemala
Activist

Rigoberta has fought for women's rights and for the rights of indigenous people in Guatemala since she was a teenager. She was forced to leave her country at the age of 21, but she continued to speak out. She made sure people around the world knew what was happening in her country and returned home to promote peace and support her people. She was awarded the Nobel Peace Prize in 1992.

SIMÓN BOLÍVAR
The Liberator Award

Born: 1783 Died: 1830, Venezuela
Military and political leader

Simón was born in Venezuela, a South American country ruled by Spanish invaders. He managed to free his country from Spanish rule, and he drove the Spanish out of Ecuador, Peru, Colombia, and Bolivia too. Bolivia is even named after him!

MUHAMMAD ALI
The Ultimate Fighter Award

Born: 1942 Died: 2016, USA
Boxer, activist

Muhammad began training as a boxer when he was 12 and won his first Olympic medal at the age of 18. He was one of the best boxers of the 20th century, but he was just as famous for campaigning against racism and war. He became an icon of pride and strength for African Americans.

ROSA PARKS
The Act of Defiance Award

Born: 1913 Died: 2005, USA
Activist

Rosa became famous in 1955 after refusing to give up her bus seat to a white passenger. At the time, black people in America were treated unfairly and Rosa was arrested and fined for what she did. Her actions helped start the civil rights movement, which eventually gave black people the same legal rights as white people.

DAVID BOWIE

Born: 1947 Died: 2016, UK/USA
Rock star, songwriter, actor

David was born as David Jones in 1947. As a boy, he wasn't afraid to be different—he wore his hair long even though people made fun of him.

He left school at 16, determined to become a musician. At first, his career looked like it was going nowhere, so David experimented with different kinds of art—he was a painter, an actor, and a mime artist. He started to call himself David Bowie, and in 1969, when he was 22, he released a single called "Space Oddity" about an astronaut called Major Tom. It became a huge success and was used on television when the first people landed on the moon. His first album, *The Man Who Sold the World*, was released a year later and made him a star.

But David wasn't just famous for his music—he was loved for his creativity. He created characters and wore wild outfits and makeup. He never stuck with one style of music or one look for long, and he inspired his fans to express themselves and be proud of their differences.

David released his final album, *Blackstar*, on January 8, 2016, his 69th birthday. It was just as daring as his early work. Two days later, David died from cancer. One of his friends wrote that *Blackstar* had been "his parting gift."

"I don't know where I'm going from here, but I promise it won't be boring." —David Bowie

THE EXPRESS YOURSELF AWARD IS GIVEN TO DAVID BOWIE FOR:

 Creating incredible music for 50 years.

Constantly challenging himself and changing his music and his look.

 Revolutionizing music and pop culture.

 Daring to be different and inspiring his fans to express themselves and be creative.

ANNE FRANK

Born: 1929 Died: 1945, Germany/Netherlands
Writer

Anne was born in Germany, to a Jewish family. When she was three, a man named Hitler took over the country. Hitler stirred up hatred and passed laws against Jewish people. So Anne's father, Otto, decided to move the family to Amsterdam, in the Netherlands.

In 1939, World War II broke out, and a year later, when Anne was 11, Hitler invaded the Netherlands. Life became even harder for Jewish people, so when Anne was 13, the family moved into a hidden part of a building behind Otto's work place, which they called the Secret Annex. They stayed there for nearly two years and couldn't go outside at all. Anne wrote in her diary, confiding her hopes, dreams, and fears. She longed to be a published writer when she grew up.

On August 4, 1944, the Nazi police discovered the Franks and took them to a concentration camp. They lived in terrible conditions. In March 1945, first Margot and then Anne died from weakness, starvation, and disease. Anne was only 15. Otto was the only member of the family to survive. He found Anne's diary and published it. It's now read by children around the world.

"Everyone has inside of them a piece of good news. The good news is that you don't know how great you can be!" —Anne Frank

THE MOST-LOVED DIARY AWARD IS GIVEN TO ANNE FRANK FOR:

 Writing beautifully and powerfully about her life.

Being brave even though she was forced to live in hiding.

 Having faith and hope in the world.

 Recording what happened to her family and other Jewish people and teaching the world about the horrors of the Holocaust.

For her 13th birthday, Anne's parents gave her a diary. Anne decided to write her entries to an imaginary friend named Kitty.

I hope I will be able to confide everything to you as I have never been able to confide in anyone, and I hope you will be a great source of comfort and support.

Anne loved films. She decorated her bedroom in the Secret Annex with postcards and pictures of movie stars.

After Anne's death, Otto had her diary published as The Diary of a Young Girl. *The book has now been published in 67 languages and has sold over 30 million copies.*

The Secret Annex is now a museum, drawing millions of visitors each year, and there is a statue of Anne not far from the house.

CONFUCIUS

Born: 551 BC Died: 479 BC, China
Teacher, politician, philosopher

Confucius's father died when he was three, and he was brought up by his mother. No one knows much about his childhood, but his family was probably very poor. He definitely loved learning, though!

Confucius eventually became a teacher. He believed that everyone should have the right to an education, no matter what their background. His Golden Rule was that people shouldn't do things to other people that they wouldn't want other people to do to them. He thought rulers should remember this too, and that they should lead by example.

At the age of 50, Confucius became a governor of a small town, eventually working his way up to one of the top jobs in government. But at the age of 56, he left his job, disappointed that the rulers of the day weren't interested in his ideas. He continued to teach, and his message and ideas spread around the country. Eventually, they were adopted by the government. He is remembered today as the most important teacher and philosopher in Chinese history.

The **WISDOM** *Award*

"When you see a worthy person, try to be like him. When you see an unworthy person, then examine your inner self." —Confucius

THE WISDOM AWARD IS GIVEN TO CONFUCIUS FOR:

Being the first teacher in China who wanted to make education possible for everyone, not just for the children of rich nobles.

Devoting his life to helping improve society and the lives of others.

Teaching that leaders should be humble and treat people with kindness.

Changing Chinese culture forever.

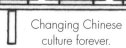

At the age of 15, Confucius realized he wanted to devote his life to learning. By his thirties, Confucius had mastered what were known as the "Six Arts"—Chinese ritual, music, archery, riding a chariot, calligraphy, and arithmetic, as well as poetry and history.

At the age of 56, Confucius left home and lived away for 12 years, surrounded by his students.

When Confucius returned home, he began to write down his ideas, so that they would live on after his death.

CLEOPATRA

Born: 69 BC Died: 30 BC, Egypt
Pharaoh of Egypt

Cleopatra came to the throne when she was 18, ruling alongside her brother, Ptolemy XIII, who was just ten. At first, Cleopatra did most of the ruling, but as Ptolemy grew older, he wanted all the power for himself and forced his sister from the throne.

Then Julius Caesar, the Roman leader, arrived in Egypt. Caesar was dazzled by Cleopatra and agreed to help her fight her brother. They won, and Cleopatra once again became ruler of Egypt. Soon after, Cleopatra and Caesar fell in love and went to live in Rome. They had a baby boy, Caesarion. But four years later, Caesar was murdered. Cleopatra returned to Egypt, but she wanted Caesarian to grow up to become ruler of Rome. One man, Octavian, stood in her way.

Cleopatra fell in love with a Roman general named Mark Antony. They joined forces and fought against Octavian in a great sea battle. Cleopatra led several warships into battle. But she and Mark Antony were defeated. Mark Antony killed himself, and when Cleopatra heard about his death, she also took her own life. Legend says she allowed herself to be bitten by venomous snakes.

"The barge she sat in, like a burnish'd throne, Burnt on the water." —*from Shakespeare's play*
Antony & Cleopatra

THE FINAL PHARAOH AWARD IS GIVEN TO CLEOPATRA FOR:

Being the last of all the pharaohs of ancient Egypt, before the country became part of the Roman empire.

Impressing people with her intelligence. Cleopatra could speak up to seven languages.

Knowing that she had just as much right to rule as her brother did and not giving in when he seized power from her.

Being a brilliant politician and winning the support of Roman leaders.

PELÉ

Born: 1940, Brazil
Soccer player

Edson Arantes do Nascimento was given his nickname "Pelé" at school. His family was very poor and couldn't afford a soccer ball, so Pelé and his friends played with balls made of socks stuffed with rags.

As a teenager, Pelé joined a youth squad. They were coached by a Brazilian soccer player who recognized Pelé's talent, and he persuaded Pelé's family to let him try out for the Santos, a professional soccer club. Pelé immediately began showing his amazing skill, becoming the top scorer in the league. He was recruited to play for the Brazilian national team, and at the age of 17, he rose to fame at the 1958 World Cup, scoring three goals in the semifinal and two more in the final, helping Brazil beat Sweden.

Pelé retired from soccer in 1977. A year later, he was awarded the International Peace Award for his work with UNICEF. He has also worked as a United Nations ambassador for the environment. Today he is known as being one of the best ever soccer players and for speaking out about the rights and living standards of poor people in Brazil.

The 1,279 GOALS Award

"The more difficult the victory, the greater the happiness in winning." —Pelé

THE 1,279 GOALS AWARD IS GIVEN TO PELÉ FOR:

Helping Brazil win the World Cup three times, in 1958, 1962, and 1970.

Being the youngest player ever to win a World Cup.

Scoring 1,279 goals in 1,363 games, including 12 in the World Cup.

His lightning speed, ball control, and spectacular goals.

As a young boy, Pelé was coached by his father, Dondinho, who had played soccer for small clubs before he was forced to stop because of an injury.

Pelé's first goal in the 1958 World Cup is often listed as one of the best goals in the history of the World Cup. He flicked the ball over a defender before volleying it into the corner of the net.

In 1975, Pele was offered a multi-million contract to play for a team called the New York Cosmos. It made him one of the highest-paid athletes of his time and he helped make soccer more popular in the United States.

In 2000, Pelé was voted as the Player of the Century by the International Federation of Football History & Statistics.

The nominations are in for the Inspiration Awards. These people didn't just achieve great things themselves—they inspired others to try harder, to keep going, and to believe in themselves. They are still inspiring people today!

ANA NZINGA
The Warrior Queen Award

Born: c. 1583 Died: 1663, Angola
Ruler of the Ndongo and Matamba Kingdoms (modern-day Angola)

Queen Nzinga ruled at a time when the Portuguese were trying to take over large parts of Africa and sell African people into slavery. Unlike other rulers of the time, Queen Nzinga refused to give in to the Portuguese and instead fought for the freedom of her people.

DONALD BRADMAN
The Sports Legend Award

Born: 1908 Died: 2001, Australia
Cricketer

As a young boy, Donald practised cricket for hours on his own, hitting a ball against a wall using a cricket stump as a bat. He left school at 14 and worked as an estate agent, but by the age of 20, he was playing for his country. He set many records for top scoring, and he is thought of as the greatest ever batsman.

EVA PERÓN
The First Lady Award

Born: 1919 Died: 1952, Argentina
Actress, politician

Eva grew up in a poor family and left home at 15 to become an actress. Then, in 1945, she married Juan Perón, who went on to become president of Argentina. Eva, nicknamed "Evita," used her position as first lady to speak out and help poor people in Argentina and to fight for women's rights.

JOAN OF ARC
The Rebel Teen Award

Born: 1412 Died: 1431, France
Military leader

As a young girl, Joan of Arc had visions of an angel telling her to lead the French in battle against the English, who were trying to conquer the country. So when she was 16, she asked the French king if she could lead an army into battle. He agreed. She led the French troops to an amazing victory. Joan is remembered as a heroine of France.

LUDWIG VAN BEETHOVEN

Born: 1770 Died: 1827, Germany/Austria
Pianist, composer

Ludwig was born in Germany. His father wanted him to be a famous child pianist, so he forced him to practice for hours and beat him if he made a mistake.

When Ludwig was 16, he traveled to Vienna in Austria to study with Mozart—but he had to return home because his mother was seriously ill. She died shortly afterward. Beethoven had to care for his younger brothers for the next five years.

In 1792, Ludwig returned to Vienna. He became famous for his amazing talent on the piano—and also for his temper. He would stop performing if the audience talked or didn't pay enough attention. Then Ludwig began to lose his hearing. By the age of 30, he was so deaf he had to give up his career as a pianist and focus on composing. He wrote music by imagining how it would sound.

Ludwig reimagined what classical music could be, changing the way people composed and played music forever. He wrote nine symphonies (music for all the instruments in an orchestra), as well as choral music, piano music, string quartets, and an opera. He is thought of as one of the greatest classical composers of all time.

The **BAD-TEMPERED MUSICAL GENIUS** *Award*

"Don't only practice your art, but force your way into its secrets." —*Ludwig Van Beethoven*

THE BAD-TEMPERED MUSICAL GENIUS AWARD IS GIVEN TO BEETHOVEN FOR:

Being so bad-tempered that he fought with his brothers, his publishers, his housekeepers, and his pupils.

Constantly pushing himself to learn new things.

Reinventing music with every new piece he composed.

Writing incredible pieces of music including the *Moonlight Sonata*, *Appassionata*, and his *Ninth Symphony*.

At first, Ludwig was so small he needed a footstool to reach the piano keys.

Ludwig had his first symphony performed when he was
30, at the Burgtheater in Vienna.

In 1802, filled with despair at his deafness, Ludwig wrote (but never sent) a letter to his brothers, telling them how much he suffered,
but that he was determined to keep going for the sake of his music.

MARIA MONTESSORI

Born: 1870 Died: 1952, Italy
Doctor, teacher

When Maria was growing up, many people thought women couldn't do the same jobs as men. But she never let that stop her. When she left school, she became one of Italy's first female doctors.

Maria began working with children with learning disabilities. She studied how children learned and tried out new ways of teaching. In 1907, she opened her first school in a poor area of Rome. There, she developed her idea that the teacher should "follow the child." She wanted teachers to find out what children were interested in and use this to help them learn. Two years later, Maria set up her own training course for teachers and wrote a book about her way of education.

But then, in the 1930s, Hitler came to power in Germany and Mussolini became the new ruler in Italy. They shut down Maria's schools and ordered her books to be burned. Maria was forced out of Italy until the end of World War II. When she returned, she started teaching peace education in her schools.

Maria's style of teaching is still used all over the world today. There are more than 22,000 Montessori schools in 110 countries.

The Children's Champion Award

"The child is both a hope and a promise for mankind."
—*Maria Montessori*

THE CHILDREN'S CHAMPION AWARD IS GIVEN TO MARIA MONTESSORI FOR:

Finding new ways to teach children with disabilities.

Changing how children are educated around the world.

Being nominated for the Nobel Peace Prize three times.

Encouraging teachers to treat children as individuals.

At Maria's first Montessori school, the Casa dei Bambini, the children were encouraged to do puzzles, cook meals, and learn maths by playing with objects. Maria believed that through play, children could teach themselves.

Maria traveled all over the world, speaking out about education and women's rights. She kept working and campaigning all her life.

When World War Two broke out, Maria was in India with her son, Mario, and couldn't return home. She stayed for seven years and taught the Montessori method to over a thousand Indian teachers.

TEGLA LOROUPE

Born: 1973, Kenya
Long-distance runner, United Nations Ambassador for Sports

Tegla grew up in a village in Kenya with 24 brothers and sisters. She spent much of her childhood working in the fields and caring for her siblings. She was nicknamed "Chametia," meaning "the one who never gets annoyed."

Tegla's talent for running was spotted at school races, but her father told her that running was unladylike and that she should become a babysitter instead. Tegla nearly gave up on her dreams.

At first, the people in charge of Kenya's running team thought Tegla was too small to be a champion. But then, at age 15, she won an important barefoot race. After that, Tegla ran in competitions all over the world, only wearing shoes when the ground was very rough. In 1994, she became the first African woman to win the New York City Marathon.

Tegla went on to win many more major marathons. She became famous around the world and decided to help the community she grew up in. She started a foundation to promote peace and women's rights and founded the Tegla Loroupe Peace Race in which warriors from warring tribes lay down their weapons and run together.

The **INSPIRING RUNNER** *Award*

"I think I have the strength to prove that even small people can do something big."
—Tegla Loroupe

THE INSPIRING RUNNER AWARD IS GIVEN TO TEGLA LOROUPE FOR:

Running more than 6 miles to and from school every morning from the age of seven.

Holding the world records for the fastest 20 km, 25 km, and 30 km.

Founding the Tegla Loroupe Peace Foundation to promote women's rights and bring peace to the community she grew up in.

Helping organize the first ever Refugee Team for the 2016 Summer Olympics.

MALALA YOUSAFZAI

Born: 1997, Pakistan/UK
Activist, student

Malala grew up in Swat Valley, Pakistan. Girls in Pakistan had fewer opportunities than boys, but Malala's father was determined that she should have a good education.

When Malala was ten, a group known as the Taliban took over the area where she lived. They banned television and killed people who didn't obey them. They also banned girls from going to school. Using a different name, Malala began blogging about what life was like under the Taliban.

When she was 14, the Pakistani army forced the Taliban to retreat. At last, Malala could go back to school. She spoke out about the importance of education for girls and became well known around the world. The Taliban wanted to silence her. On October 9, 2012, a gunman boarded her school bus and shot her. Malala was flown to a hospital in the UK. After months of treatment, she was finally able to leave the hospital.

On her 16th birthday, Malala spoke at the United Nations. The UN declared the day "Malala Day." She continued her studies and won a place at Oxford, one of the world's best universities. She still campaigns for girls everywhere to get an education.

"When the whole world is silent, even one voice becomes powerful."
—*Malala Yousafzai*

THE ONE VOICE AWARD IS GIVEN TO MALALA YOUSAFZAI FOR:

Speaking out about a girl's right to be educated, even at the risk of her own life.

Believing that her voice could make a difference.

Writing a book: *I Am Malala: The Story of the Girl Who Stood Up for Education and Was Shot by the Taliban.*

Continuing to speak out and campaign for girls' and women's rights, even after being shot.

When she was 11, Malala's father took her to a local journalism club, where she stood up and spoke out against the Taliban regime, which was blowing up girls' schools in Swat Valley.

In December 2014, Malala won the Nobel Peace Prize, becoming the youngest ever person to win. She invited girls from Syria, Nigeria, and Pakistan to attend the ceremony with her.

Malala marked her 18th birthday by opening a secondary school for Syrian refugee girls in Lebanon's Bekaa Valley.

THE LAP OF HONOR

It's time for our award winners to take a bow! Have a look at this timeline to find out who lived when.

SAPPHO
A great poet of ancient times

c. 630 BC–c.580 BC

CONFUCIUS
Chinese philosopher and teacher

551 BC–479 BC

CLEOPATRA
Ruler of ancient Egypt

69 BC–30 BC

SEJONG THE GREAT
A king who invented the Korean alphabet

1397-1450

JOAN OF ARC
Led the French army to victory during the Hundred Years' War

1412–1431

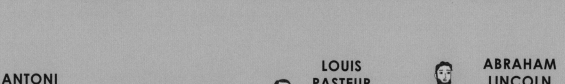

ANTONI GAUDÍ
Spanish architect

1852–1926

ALFRED NOBEL
Scientist who set up the Nobel Prizes

1833–1896

LOUIS PASTEUR
Scientist who developed the first vaccines

1822–1895

ABRAHAM LINCOLN
President of the United States who abolished slavery

1809–1865

HANS CHRISTIAN ANDERSEN
Author of some of the world's most famous fairy tales

1805–1875

MARIE CURIE
Scientist who made important discoveries about radioactivity

1867–1934

MAHATMAGANDHI
Great and peaceful Indian leader

1869–1948

MARIA MONTESSORI
Doctor and teacher who invented the Montessori method

1870–1952

ROALD AMUNDSEN
The first person to reach the South Pole

1872–1928

ALBERT EINSTEIN
Scientist who came up with the world's most famous equation, $E=mc^2$

1879–1955

PELÉ
Brazilian soccer player

Born 1940

WANGARI MAATHAI
Kenyan activist and founder of the Green Belt Movement

1940–2011

RUDOLF NUREYEV
Russian dancer and choreographer

1938–1993

VALENTINA TERESHKOVA
Russian cosmonaut and the first woman to fly into space

Born 1937

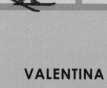

ANNE FRANK
Writer and diarist

1929–1945

MUHAMMAD ALI
Boxer and political activist

1942–2016

ERNÖ RUBIK
Inventor of the Rubik's cube

Born 1944

DAVID BOWIE
Singer, songwriter, and actor

1947–2016

TIM BERNERS-LEE
Inventor of the World Wide Web

Born 1955

ELLEN DEGENERES
Comedian, television host, actress, and writer

Born 1958

LEONARDO DA VINCI
Italian painter, sculptor, architect, and inventor

1452–1519

ANTÓNIA RODRIGUES
Portuguese knight

1580–1641

ANA NZINGA
African queen who fought for the freedom of her people

1583–1663

JAN AMOS KOMENSKÝ
Teacher and educator

1592–1670

ISAAC NEWTON
Scientist, mathematician, and astronomer

1643–1727

MARY ANNING
Fossil hunter

1799–1847

SIMÓN BOLÍVAR
Freed South American countries from Spanish rule

1783–1830

LUDWIG VAN BEETHOVEN
German composer

1770–1827

WOLFGANG AMADEUS MOZART
Austrian composer

1756–1791

OLAUDAH EQUIANO
Former slave who wrote a bestselling book about his life

1745–1797

PABLO PICASSO
Spanish artist

1881–1973

FRIDA KAHLO
Mexican artist

1907–1954

DONALD BRADMAN
Australian cricketer

1908–2001

ROSA PARKS
American civil fights activist

1913–2005

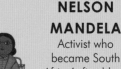

NELSON MANDELA
Activist who became South Africa's first black president

1918–2013

GABRIEL GARCÍA MÁRQUEZ
Colombian writer

1927–2014

HANAE MORI
Japanese fashion designer

Born 1926

VINCENT LINGIARI
Aboriginal rights activist

1919–1988

EVA PERÓN
First lady of Argentina

1919–1952

KATHERINE JOHNSON
NASA physicist and mathematician

Born 1918

RIGOBERTA MENCHÚ TUM
Guatemalan political activist

Born 1959

TRISCHA ZORN
Record-breaking American Paralympian

Born 1964

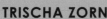

J. K. ROWLING
Author of the Harry Potter books

Born 1965

TEGLA LOROUPE
Kenyan long-distance runner

Born 1973

MALALA YOUSAFZAI
Pakistani human right's activist and the youngest Nobel Prize winner

Born 1997